WONDERS OF THE WORLD

Bristlecone Pines

Kelli M. Brucken

KIDHAVEN PRESS

An imprint of Thomson Gale, a part of The Thomson Corporation

THOMSON

GALE™

Detroit • New York • San Francisco • San Diego • New Haven, Conn.
Waterville, Maine • London • Munich

LIBRARY OF CONGRESS CATALOGING-IN-PUBLICATION DATA

Brucken, Kelli M., 1974-
  Bristlecone pines / by Kelli M. Brucken.
    p. cm. — (Wonders of the world)
  Includes bibliographical references.
  ISBN 0-7377-3061-7 (hardcover : alk. paper) 1. Rocky Mountain bristlecone pine—Juvenile literature. I. Title. II. Wonders of the world (KidHaven Press).
  QK494.5.P66B78 2005
  585'.2—dc22
                                                                  2005007770

CONTENTS

4   CHAPTER ONE
The Amazing Bristlecone Pines

16   CHAPTER TWO
The Discovery of the Bristlecone's
Ancient Heritage

27   CHAPTER THREE
Protecting the Bristlecone Pines

35   CHAPTER FOUR
The Future of North America's Oldest Tree

44   Glossary

45   For Further Exploration

46   Index

48   Picture Credits

48   About the Author

The Amazing Bristlecone Pines

Bristlecone pines are the oldest trees in the world. They have grown high on windswept mountaintops for thousands of years. The pines were seedlings when the ancient Egyptians built the pyramids. From Colorado to California, these ancient trees stand as living links to the past.

Bristlecone pine trees survive in the harshest of living conditions. In winter they are scoured by windblown ice crystals and stand buried in snow. In summer they bake in the fierce sun, parched by the hot, dry air. They live on a scant 10 to 12 inches (25 to 31 centimeters) of moisture a year. Most of this is in the form of snow.

Bristlecone pines are unusually beautiful. Their gnarled and twisted branches are the result of constant battering from fierce mountain winds. Their multiple

The gnarled roots and twisted branches of bristlecone pines are the result of the extremely harsh conditions in which they grow.

trunks twist together to form a strong barrier against the elements. The bristlecones' bark is deep red brown and lined with thick, scaly ridges. The crown of the tree is spiky, bursting with deep-green needles.

Needles 1 to 1.5 inches (2.5 to 3.8 centimeters) long sprout from the branches in groups of five. This gives

Red in color, these male pine cones (close-up, inset) will take about two years to fully develop.

the tree the appearance of a bottlebrush. The needles are tickly soft when stroked downward, but prickle like a cactus when rubbed in the opposite direction. The ends of the branches sport the trees' flowers, or pinecones.

Both female and male trees produce cones. The cones take two years to mature to a length of about 2.5 to 3.8 inches (6.4 to 9.7 centimeters). With an **ovoid** or egglike shape, male cones are red-purple in color. The female cones are a deeper purple-brown. The name *bristlecone* comes from the clawlike bristles on the tips of the female cones' scales.

There are two different species of bristlecones. In 1970 amateur botanist Dana K. Bailey discovered slight differences in the needles and cones of bristlecones that grew in the eastern part of the

The clawlike bristles on the tips of the female cones' scales give bristlecone pines their name.

United States versus the western part. Due to Bailey's findings, new species names were created. Pinus aristata, or the Rocky Mountain bristlecones, grow in Colorado, Arizona, and New Mexico. Pinus longaeva, or the Great Basin bristlecones, grow in California, Nevada, and Utah.

Survival of the Fittest

Bristlecone pine trees put more energy into surviving than growing tall. The tallest trees can grow to around

Types of Bristlecone Pines

Pinus aristata
(Rocky Mountain Bristlecone Pines)

Pinus longaeva
(Great Basin Bristlecone Pines)

Rocky Mountain bristlecone pines are taller, thinner, and less twisted than the Great Basin variety. Rocky Mountain pine needles also have eight to twelve tiny dots of white sap, which is not found on the Great Basin bristlecone pines.

60 feet (18 meters), but most do not reach that height. Even with multistemmed trunks, many of the trees are not massive in width. The trunks of younger trees often are no wider than 6 or 7 feet (1.8 to 2.1 meters). As the trees grow older, however, their trunks expand.

With seven twisted stems forming its trunk, the fattest bristlecone is called the Patriarch. At a height of only 41 feet (12.5 meters), the Patriarch is around 36 feet (11

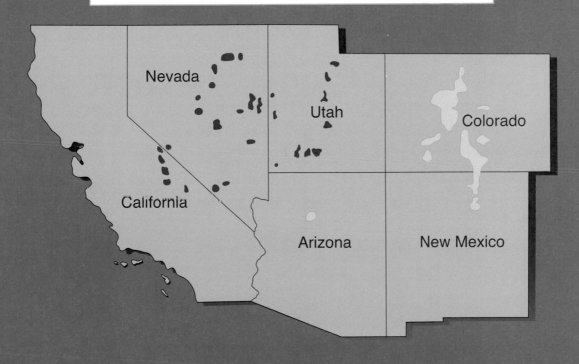

Where Bristlecone Pines Are Found

Nevada

Utah

Colorado

California

Arizona

New Mexico

Pinus longaeva
(Great Basin Bristlecone Pines)

Pinus aristata
(Rocky Mountain Bristlecone Pines)

meters) wide. The tree stands in the Ancient Bristlecone Pine Forest in the White Mountains of California. It was named in 1947 by a U.S. Forest Service district ranger. *Patriarch* means "father" or "chief of a race."

Because they live in such a harsh environment, survival is the bristlecone pines' first priority. They have adapted beautifully to their plight and have created some amazing ways to survive.

Survival Tips

Bristlecone pine trees thrive in poor soil mixed with **dolomite**. Dolomite is a type of mineral that is formed in rocks. It has few nutrients but holds water well. The light-colored dolomite crystals also reflect sunlight better than other rocks do. This helps keep the ground cool, which helps the trees save moisture at their roots.

Bristlecones have long, shallow roots that maximize water absorption. The trees are also rich in **resin**, or sap, which seeps from the trees. The sap oozes over branches, forming a waterproof barrier that holds in precious moisture.

Conserving energy is another important aspect of the bristlecones' survival. The trees do not drop their waxy needles each year. Instead the same needles may be on the tree for twenty to thirty years. Producing new needles every growing season would take a lot of nutrients and energy.

Bristlecones also grow very slowly, averaging only 1 inch (2.5 centimeters) every one hundred years. In the summer months, if the weather is good, they grow for a short six to eight weeks. If the trees face drought, extreme winds, or other harsh weather conditions during their growth period, however, they might not grow at all.

The bristlecone pine's most amazing survival trait is its unusual ability to let part of its trunk or branches die. If a root or branch of the tree is damaged by fire, drought, or storms, the tree simply lets the affected part die off. This helps reduce the amount of nutrients needed to keep the remaining branches healthy. A lot of

This enormous bristlecone pine grows in the Ancient Bristlecone Pine Forest in California. It is known as the Patriarch, which means "father."

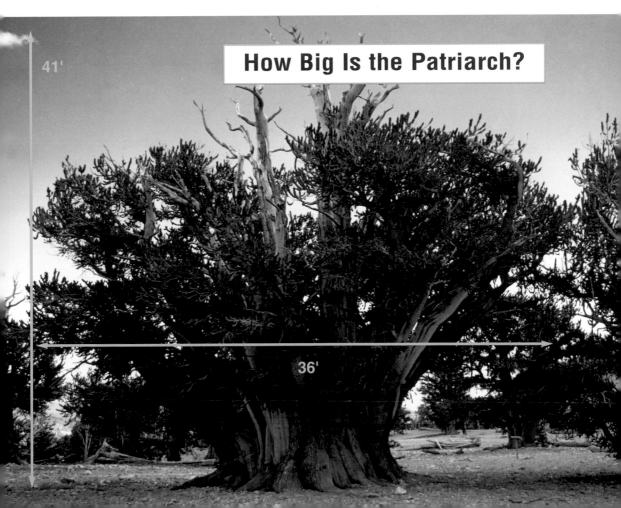

41'

How Big Is the Patriarch?

36'

bristlecone pines, in fact, are mostly dead wood. They have only a narrow strip of living bark that connects the crown to the roots.

The bristlecone's dense wood and thick resin also help it avoid attacks from bacteria and insects. The cool, dry air of the mountains lessens fungi, which causes rot.

Even after all the living tissue in a bristlecone pine has died, the tree can still stand for hundreds of years. Eventually the supporting roots may decay or the ground around the roots may erode, causing the tree to fall.

Because bristlecone pines live where practically nothing else can survive, the trees do not have to compete for the few existing nutrients and moisture. The trees grow with plenty of space between them. This reduces the chance of a wildfire hopping from tree to tree and spreading throughout an entire grove. When bristlecones reproduce, they need the help of a particular bird.

Feathered Friends

In order for seeds to produce new bristlecone pines, they must find a way into the ground. A bird called the Clark's nutcracker plays an important role in dispersing bristlecone pine seeds.

At about 11 inches (28 centimeters) in length, a Clark's nutcracker is not a large bird. However, its long, pointed bill is tremendously strong. It uses this crowbarlike bill to pry open and crack the hard cones of pine trees, getting to the tasty seeds inside.

During the late summer and fall, when pine seeds are ripe, this busy bird can collect and store between twenty

The Clark's nutcracker helps spread bristlecone pine seeds as it collects up to 30,000 seeds throughout the year.

Capable of surviving the harshest conditions imaginable, the ancient bristlecone pines are true wonders of the world.

thousand and thirty thousand seeds. The bird has a special pouch, located under its tongue, in which it carries the seeds. It can stuff up to ninety-five seeds in its pouch at one time.

When its pouch is full, the bird finds a hiding spot for the seeds. It digs through the earth with its strong beak and makes a hole to bury the seeds underground. This collection of seeds is called a **cache**. Throughout the winter, spring, and summer, the bird returns to its caches to feed on its hidden meals. A Clark's nutcracker will even dig through snow to reach its treasure. It has a great memory and can remember the location of more than one thousand different caches over one year. Some caches are forgotten, however. It is these seeds, protected in a nutcracker hole, that may grow to become new bristlecone pines.

Against all odds, the amazing bristlecone pines have survived. They have stood on high mountaintops as the world changed around them. Through floods and droughts, blizzards, and storms, they will stand, connecting the present to the past.

CHAPTER TWO

The Discovery of the Bristlecone's Ancient Heritage

Before the discovery of the bristlecone pine, it was thought that the tallest trees in the world—the giant sequoias—were also the oldest. That all changed with the findings of one man.

Bristlecone pines, like most trees, usually add one growth ring to their trunk each year. In the spring, when the growing season starts, a tree puts all its energy into making new growth cells. These first cells are large. As the season goes on, the tree's energy level lowers, and the cells get smaller. This continues until all growth stops at the end of the season. The next year, when the growing season starts again, the tree makes more new large cells. The size difference between these large and small cells makes a visible growth ring inside the tree's trunk.

Lifespan of a Bristlecone Pine

By counting the hundreds of tree rings in the cross section of this ancient bristlecone pine, scientists discovered that this tree lived from 900 B.C. to 1956, and was alive during some of the major events in the history of humankind.

Birth of Jesus – A.D. 1

900 B.C.

Columbus Arrives in the Americas – 1492

1956

The Middle Ages Begin – 1066

World War I Begins – 1914

Declaration of Independence – 1776

In 1957 dendrochronologist Edmund Schulman discovered a bristlecone pine that was nearly 5,000 years old.

Dendrochronology is the study of tree growth rings. *Dendro* means "tree," and *chronology* means "time." Dendrochronologists are scientists who study tree growth rings to get a picture of how the Earth has changed over time.

In 1953 Edmund Schulman was a dendrochronologist at the University of Arizona's Laboratory of Tree-Ring Research. For twenty years Schulman had been studying how the climate affected tree growth rings. He was trying to make a complete historical weather record for all of western America. At the time, weather records went back only a few centuries. It was Schulman's plan, through tree-ring research, to extend that record as far into the past as he could.

By studying pine trees such as the pinyon and douglas fir, Schulman had found trees with growth rings that dated back between eight hundred and one thousand years. Then he heard from a man named Al Noren.

Noren was a ranger at Inyo National Forest in the White Mountains of California. After taking some bristlecone pine wood home to use as paneling in his house, Noren noticed the wood showed many growth rings. When he looked at the rings under a microscope, Noren realized he had found some very old wood. As a follower of Schulman's work, Noren thought the dendrochronologist would be interested in the sample. Although Schulman was skeptical, he decided to visit the White Mountain bristlecone pines.

On Schulman's first visit to the White Mountains, he came across the Patriarch. Intrigued, he used a tool called a borer to take a pencil-thin core from the center of the tree's trunk.

A borer is a long, skinny hand tool with a hollow shaft. The shaft is screwed into the tree. An extractor, which is similar to a long spoon, is inserted into the shaft and used to pull out a core sample. The tree's resin oozes into the hole left by the borer. Within a year or so, the tree is healed.

Schulman viewed his sample from the Patriarch under a microscope. He measured, examined, and recorded each ring and found the tree to be fifteen hundred years old. This was exciting news!

Schulman was even more excited when he found that the bristlecone pine's growth rings showed extreme sensitivity to changing weather conditions. That meant environmental differences altered the size and shape of the tree's rings. In dry years the rings were very narrow. In wet years the rings were wider. This convinced Schulman that he needed to focus his study on bristlecone pines.

Throughout 1954 and 1955 Schulman carried out extensive studies on the trees from Colorado to California. He discovered seventeen trees that had been living for more than four thousand years. All but one of those trees were located in the White Mountains.

Schulman named the first tree he found past the age of four thousand years, Pine Alpha. *Alpha* is the first letter of the Greek alphabet and is often used to describe something that is first, in order or in importance.

In 1957 Schulman made his most impressive find. He discovered a tree that was 4,723 years old. It was the

History of a Bristlecone Pine Tree

Each spring and summer, bristlecone pines add new layers of wood to their trunks and create new tree rings. By studying the shape, thickness, color, and evenness of the ring patterns, scientists can learn about the climate and history of the vegetation in the area.

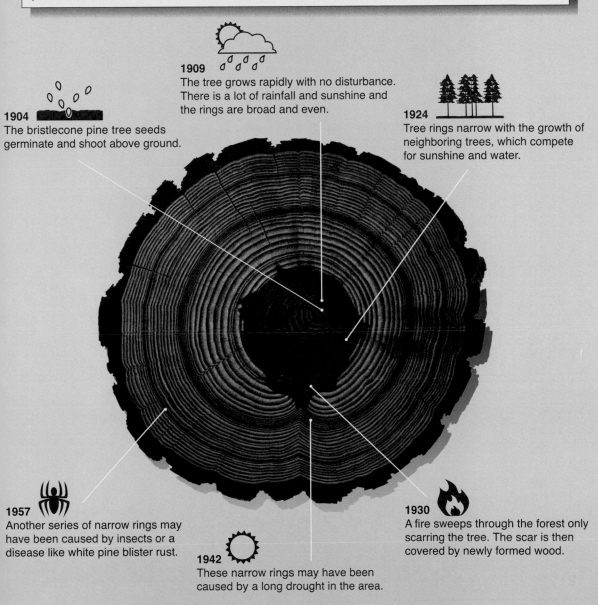

1909
The tree grows rapidly with no disturbance. There is a lot of rainfall and sunshine and the rings are broad and even.

1904
The bristlecone pine tree seeds germinate and shoot above ground.

1924
Tree rings narrow with the growth of neighboring trees, which compete for sunshine and water.

1957
Another series of narrow rings may have been caused by insects or a disease like white pine blister rust.

1942
These narrow rings may have been caused by a long drought in the area.

1930
A fire sweeps through the forest only scarring the tree. The scar is then covered by newly formed wood.

By studying the growth rings of dead and living bristlecone pines, scientists created a chronology that stretches back thousands of years.

oldest living tree that had ever been found. He named it Methuselah. In the Bible it is said that a man named Methuselah lived to be 969 years old. He has been held as a symbol of long life ever since.

Finding a tree able to live for such a long time awed Schulman. Doug Powell, Schulman's assistant in 1957, reported in a PBS special aired in 2001 that Schulman hoped to find some kind of magic potion or elixir hidden deep in the trees that was the answer to long life. Unfortunately no such potion existed, and Schulman died from a heart attack at the young age of forty-nine. Before his passing, however, he shared his findings with the world in the March 1958 issue of *National Geographic*. Schulman's discovery caught the attention of the scientific community. Scientists used core samples from live bristlecone pines to create weather records reaching back more than four thousand years.

Dead bristlecone wood proved to be just as valuable as live wood. Due to the wood's high resin content and durability, dead bristlecone wood can lay unchanged on the ground for thousands of years. Scientists discovered that they could compare and match the growth rings of dead wood to the rings of living wood. This method, which they called **cross dating**, provided them with an unbroken chronology that went back more than eight thousand years. That amazing time line helped scientists unravel yet another scientific mystery.

The Trees That Rewrote History

For a long time archaeologists did not have a scientific way to determine the age of ancient artifacts. It was

Radiocarbon Dating

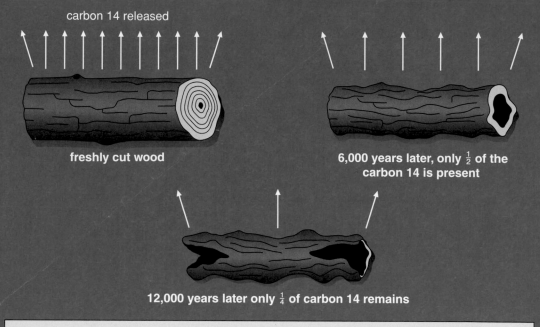

carbon 14 released

freshly cut wood

6,000 years later, only $\frac{1}{2}$ of the carbon 14 is present

12,000 years later only $\frac{1}{4}$ of carbon 14 remains

When plants or animals die, they begin to decay and release carbon 14 atoms. Scientists know that after about 6,000 years, only $\frac{1}{2}$ the carbon 14 atoms will remain, and after about 12,000 years, only $\frac{1}{4}$ will be present. By measuring the amount of carbon 14 atoms in the dead animal or tree trunk, they can work out its age.

thought that the farther underground an object was found, the older it was. When archaeologists found items close together, they assumed the artifacts were similar in age. They used other clues, such as drawings on coins or pottery, to date objects. Scientists still had a lot of unanswered questions, however. They got answers with the invention of **radiocarbon dating**.

Carbon 14 is a material that occurs naturally in the environment. When plants and animals breathe, they absorb carbon 14. When they die carbon 14 is no longer absorbed, and what is already in the body begins to decay.

Cross Dating

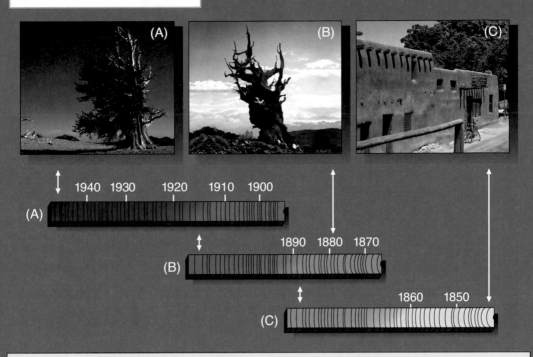

In cross dating, scientists compare the tree ring patterns in live (A) and older dead (B) bristlecone pines. They then match these patterns to those in the wood in an old building (C). By counting the rings back from the present, they can tell the age of the building.

In 1949 scientist William Libbey discovered that the amount of carbon 14 found in a dead organism could reveal how long the plant or animal had been dead. This was a giant leap for the scientific community. For the next twenty years, radiocarbon dating was used to date archaeological finds. The process could not be used on things that had never lived, such as coins or pottery. However, some type of plant or animal matter was usually found at the same archaeological site and could be tested.

Then around 1960, researchers found some ancient Egyptian **hieroglyphics** that included specific dates.

The dates showed that the age of the artifacts were far off the radiocarbon dates the researchers had recorded previously. Something was wrong, but scientists did not know what.

Bristlecone pine trees provided the answer. Scientists found that the growth rings of a bristlecone pine were a record of how much carbon 14 had been in the environment during a specific year. They discovered that the amount of carbon 14 in the atmosphere varied from year to year. It was not a steady level, as they had thought in the past.

This told scientists that carbon 14 levels in an organism would be different depending on the year it had died. The ancient Egyptian dates did not match the radiocarbon dates because scientists had assumed the amount of carbon 14 in the environment was always the same.

The longevity of the bristlecone pines gave scientists the opportunity to refine the process of radiocarbon dating. The bristlecones became known as the "trees that rewrote history" for the role they played in updating the process.

Schulman's discovery of the bristlecone's ancient heritage was one of the most important scientific finds in his field. Suddenly the world sat up and took notice of the bristlecone pines.

CHAPTER THREE

Protecting the Bristlecone Pines

Schulman's fantastic find brought much attention to the bristlecone. Scientists decided that in order to preserve bristlecone pines for research, the trees would need protection.

Forest managers at the Inyo National Forest were the first to name and regulate an official bristlecone pine area. They set aside 28,000 acres (11,331 hectares) of land as the Ancient Bristlecone Pine Forest Botanical Area. The place where the most ancient trees grew was named Schulman Grove in memory of the scientist's important contributions.

When the botanical area was formed, a special order was put in place by the Inyo National Forest supervisor. The order made it illegal to cut down or even collect dead bristlecone wood within the forest.

To Fence or Not to Fence

Some people believed these special trees needed even more protection. Linus Pauling was one of them.

Pauling was a Nobel Prize–winning scientist who shared Schulman's belief that the bristlecones would uncover a fountain of youth of sorts. He yearned to find the trees' secret to long life. He was convinced, if given the chance, the public would destroy the bristlecone pines. He wrote several letters to the United States Department of Agriculture (USDA) Forest Service proposing that a stout chain-link fence be put up around 58,000 acres (23,472 hectares) in the White Mountains to ensure a bristlecone research preserve.

Jospeh T. Randel, supervisor of the Inyo National Forest from 1955 to 1971, did not agree with Pauling's

drastic idea. Randel was positive the trees could be protected without denying the public access to the national park. Eventually Randel convinced Pauling and Forest Service officials that keeping the public out was not a good idea. It was decided that education would be the best way to protect the trees. It was the drive for education, however, that brought about one of the worst bristlecone-pine disasters in history.

The Tragedy of Prometheus

Bristlecone pines have long grown in Great Basin National Park in the Snake Mountains of Nevada. In the early 1960s a conservation group, the Great Basin National Park Association, was certain that the bristlecone pines found in the park on Wheeler Peak were as old or older than the famous bristlecones of the White Mountains. The group visited Wheeler Peak frequently and had even given the bristlecones names such as Buddha and Socrates. One tree was named Prometheus.

Bristlecone pines in the Inyo National Forest in California are protected by the National Forest Service.

In Nevada's Great Basin National Park, bristlecone pines have lived for nearly 5,000 years. A dendrochronology tag (inset) on a tree's growth rings indicates its age.

In ancient Greek mythology, Prometheus was a Titan (giant) who stole fire from Zeus, the ruler of the Greek gods, and gave it to humans. As punishment, Prometheus was chained to a mountaintop for all eternity. It is not known why the group chose that name for the tree. Perhaps they knew that Prometheus could provide great gifts of knowledge if it was studied.

The Great Basin National Park Association was determined to study Prometheus and the other bristlecones in their area. The University of Nevada showed a little interest in the project but did not see it through. The Board of National Parks introduced bills to both houses of Congress to support bristlecone study on Wheeler Peak. But the legislation failed year after year.

Finally in 1964, someone did come to study the bristlecones of Wheeler Peak. Unfortunately the research was

Two dead bristlecone pines stand on the Schulman Discovery Trail in the Inyo National Forest. Schulman's research helped convince scientists that bristlecones should be protected.

not done in a way the conservation group would have wanted.

Don Currey was a graduate student of geography at the University of North Carolina. When his mother sent him a copy of Schulman's *National Geographic* article on bristlecone pines, he became interested in the mystery of the trees.

As part of his graduate studies, Currey traveled to Wheeler Peak in search of evidence of Ice Age glaciers. He was excited when he discovered that bristlecone pines grew in the area. Having read Schulman's article, Currey thought the bristlecones could help him date the glacier deposits he had found in Nevada.

When Currey came across one particularly old looking tree, he decided to take some samples. He ran into a problem, however. The largest available coring tool was too small to do the job. Not being the most experienced at taking tree samples, Currey was unsure what to do.

After some thought, he contacted the USDA Forest Service and received permission to cut the tree down. After the tree was felled, Currey took a large cross section back to his hotel for further study.

As he counted the rings under a microscope, Currey reached 4,000 years, then 4,500, then over 4,700. That was past the age of the famed Methuselah tree. Currey kept counting. When he reached more than 4,800 rings, the horror of what he had done hit him. He had found the most ancient tree in the world, and he had killed it. That tree was Prometheus.

It took some time for the news of the Prometheus tragedy to spread across the country—but it did. The Forest Service found itself with so many protesters, it had to do something. It was time to tighten up bristlecone security.

Protective Legislation

The Wilderness Act of 1964 began to provide many bristlecones with protection. The act created the legal

Protective legislation for bristlecone pines ensures that these hikers and others will enjoy these trees for many generations.

classification of a wilderness area. It defined *wilderness* as "areas administered for the use and enjoyment of the American people in such a manner as will leave them unimpaired for future use and enjoyment . . . where earth and its community of life are untrammeled by man, where man is a visitor and does not remain."

The enforcement of the act was left up to the administration of the individual wilderness areas. Following the example set at Inyo National Park, it was deemed unlawful to remove any living or dead bristlecone wood, cones, or needles from any national park or wilderness area. A stiff penalty of $5,000 or six months in jail was imposed.

The Forest Service also decided that the location of Methuselah and Pine Alpha should no longer be pointed out to the public. Too many feet trampling around the shallow roots of the trees could cause soil erosion and permanent damage. According to John Louth, current manager of the Ancient Bristlecone Pine Forest in Inyo National Park, fewer than fifty people in the world today know the actual location of the famous trees.

As the years went on, more and more people began to realize the importance of protecting the bristlecone pines. In 1987 Nevada deemed the bristlecone pine one of its official state trees. Today around 95 percent of all bristlecone pines grow on protected state or federal land.

The Future of North America's Oldest Tree

Today there are several organizations dedicated to the protection and survival of the ancient bristlecone pines. Senator Barbara Boxer from California has acted as a voice for these groups in her introduction of new legislation known as the Wild Heritage Act of 2002.

The Wild Heritage Act is a California-specific wilderness act. Its purpose is to build upon the legacy of wilderness protection initially enacted by the Wilderness Act of 1964. If passed, this act would make the protection of the bristlecone pines in California much more permanent by naming the Ancient Bristlecone Pine Forest a federally regulated wilderness area.

Other states in which the trees grow have also taken steps to protect their bristlecone pines. The Great Basin National Heritage Act was introduced in 2003. This act would provide permanent protection to the bristlecones growing in Nevada and Utah.

Cedar Breaks National Monument in Utah has established a bristlecone-pine management program to research the impact of visitor activity on the trees. A protection plan and long-term monitoring plan have

Supporters of bristlecone pines are seeking permanent federal protection for the trees in California, Nevada, and Utah.

been implemented by park employees to ensure that bristlecone pines are not lost due to human impact.

The Champion Tree Project

A nonprofit organization known as the Champion Tree Project also has taken steps to ensure the future of bristlecone pines.

The Champion Tree Project was founded in 1996 by two **arborists** from Michigan—David Milarch and his

son, Jared. The project promotes forests by cloning America's champion trees—trees that are the rarest, biggest, and oldest. The project eventually hopes to clone champions of more than eight hundred U.S. tree species.

In October 2002, the project's goal was to clone the oldest bristlecone pine on record, Methuselah. The group was granted special permission from federal officials to see the location of Methuselah and take cuttings from the ancient tree.

The mission was completed with the utmost secrecy. Lookouts were posted to watch for other hikers coming into the area. If a stranger was spotted, the group was directed to scatter

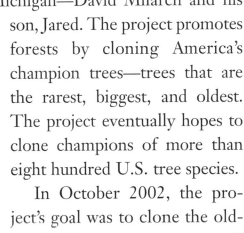

to keep the identity of Methuselah hidden. John Louth, manager of the Ancient Bristlecone Pine Forest, led the expedition that day. On a home video taken by one group member, Louth requested that no pictures of the full tree be shown. Of course, the group complied.

After reaching the famous tree, Jared Milarch took several 4- to 6-inch (10- to 15-centimeters) branch cuttings from Methuselah. He also took some pinecones as backup, in case the cloning efforts failed. The group also took cuttings from the largest bristlecone on record, the Patriarch.

As manager of the Ancient Bristlecone Pine Forest, John Louth works tirelessly to protect Methuselah, the world's oldest tree.

The cuttings were placed on ice and sent overnight to plant pathologist Chris Friel at the University of California, Davis. If the cuttings did not reach their destination in twenty-four hours, the precious cells needed for cloning would die. Thankfully, the cuttings made it in time.

It was Friel's job to plant the samples in a material rich in growth hormones. For a successful clone, the cuttings would need to grow into different parts, such as roots and branches.

Unfortunately the cloning efforts failed. The dedicated members of the Champion Tree Project did not give up. Jared Milarch extracted seeds from the pinecones he had taken from Methuselah. By planting the seeds in a special growing mixture, he was able to successfully produce eight seedlings. The only other time scientists had produced seedlings from Methuselah was in the 1970s.

LeRoy Johnson, former director of the Institute of Tree Genetics in California, led the earlier effort. His seedlings had a 100 percent **germination** rate, but they all died after being planted in unsuitable climates. That was a mistake the Milarchs hoped to avoid.

Two of the baby bristlecones that the Milarchs grew were given to the U.S. Botanical Garden in Washington, D.C. Another was given to the Strybing Arboretum in San Francisco. A network of associations called the Garden Clubs of America was given the job of finding suitable homes for the other little trees. These babies will certainly not make up a whole new bristlecone pine

David and Jared Milarch planted seedlings from cones harvested from Methuselah. The seedling in the inset is displayed in front of the U.S. Capitol in Washington, D.C.

forest, but hopefully they will help scientists unlock the trees' secret of tremendous longevity. If the secret is discovered, perhaps it could help other trees stay alive longer too.

Today, with the help of education and conservation groups, bristlecone pines that grow in national and state parks are protected from human threats. Unfortunately for the trees, they face other dangerous environmental factors.

Young bristlecone pines like these need protection.
They are vulnerable to the effects of global warming
and pollution.

Environmental Dangers

The California Native Plant Society has placed bristlecone pines on their watch list as a plant of limited distribution in California. The World Conservation Union's Species Survival Commission list bristlecone pines as vulnerable to extinction, due to present environmental conditions such as global warming and pollution.

A pair of bristlecone pines looks beautiful in the virgin snow. With proper protection, their beauty will inspire future generations of nature lovers.

Another new threat to bristlecone pines is **white pine blister rust**. This disease infects a number of five-needle pine trees, most commonly whitebark and limber pines. It is caused by a fungus that was brought into the United States from Europe in the early 1900s.

In North America the disease has caused more damage and costs more money to control than any other pine disease. In the western United States and Canada, some stands of whitebark pine have been completely destroyed by the fungus.

In 2003, for the first time ever, a bristlecone pine was infected with white pine blister rust. Scientists are extremely concerned that the fungus could cause as much damage to bristlecone pines as it has to whitebark pines. Researchers from the Rocky Mountain Research Station in Colorado hope to eliminate the fungus from bristlecone pines by finding bristlecone seedlings that are naturally resistant to the disease. They can then use those seedlings to vaccinate future bristlecone pines against the fungus.

Bristlecone pine forests are very special places. They are fragile and irreplaceable parts of the environment. The stories of the past that these trees tell us, as well as their great beauty, are too valuable to lose. With the work of environmentalists, researchers, and the public, these ancient trees will live on to tell us even more secrets of the past.

Glossary

arborists: People who specialize in treating damaged trees; tree surgeons.

cache: A hidden storage space.

chronology: A record of events in time, arranged by the order in which they occurred.

cross dating: A method for dating wooden objects that compares the tree ring patterns in live and dead wood.

dendrochronology: The branch of science that studies tree growth rings. A dendrochronologist is a scientist who specializes in the study of tree growth rings.

dolomite: A light-colored mineral containing calcium and magnesium. Dolomite rocks are similar to limestone but are made up of almost 100% dolomite crystals.

germination: The process in which seeds sprout and begin to grow.

hieroglyphics: A writing system that uses pictures.

ovoid: Oval or egg shaped.

radiocarbon dating: A process of dating organic material by calculating the amount of carbon 14 that material possesses.

resin: Any type of sticky natural substance obtained from plants.

white pine blister rust: A disease caused by the fungi rust, which damages the bark and wood of five-needle pine trees.

For Further Exploration

Books

Anna Lewington, *Ancient Trees: Trees That Live for 1,000 Years*. London, UK: Collins & Brown, 1999. A fascinating book full of wonderful photographs and exciting information on many ancient trees.

Thomas Pakenham, *Remarkable Trees of the World*. New York: W.W. Norton, 2002. This book reveals secrets of some truly amazing trees from the giants to the dwarfs.

D.M. Souza, *Wacky Trees*. New York: Franklin Watts, 2003. An exploration of many strange and wonderful trees, such as baobab, strangler fig, mangrove, and bristlecone pine.

Web Sites

Great Basin National Park (www.great.basin.national-park.com). This site provides some great information about bristlecone pines found in the park, as well as information on where and how to view the trees.

University of Arizona's Laboratory of Tree-Ring Research (http://tree.ltrr.arizona.edu/~hal/tancient.pdf). This site provides wonderful information on the ancient bristlecone pines and the science of dendrochronology.

Index

age, 4
  archaeology and, 26
  determining, 16
  of Prometheus, 29, 32
  Schulman and, 20, 23
Ancient Bristlecone Forest, 10, 27, 34, 35
appearance, 4, 6
archaeology, 23–26
artifacts, dating ancient, 23–26

bacteria, 12
Bailey, Dana K., 7
bark, 6
borers, 20
Boxer, Barbara, 35
branches, 11–12
Buddha, 29

California, 35
California Native Plant Society, 42
carbon 14, 24–26
Cedar Breaks National Monument, 36–37
Champion Tree Project, 37–39
Clark's nutcracker, 12, 14–15
cloning, 37–39
cones, 7, 38, 39
cross dating, 23, 25
Currey, Don, 32

dead wood, 11–12
dendrochronology
  archaeology and, 26
  Prometheus and, 29–32
  Schulman and, 19–20, 23
dolomite, 10

douglas firs, 19

education, 29, 31–32
energy conservation, 10
environmental dangers, 42

female cones, 7
Forest Service, 28–29, 32, 33–34
Friel, Chris, 39
fungi, 12

Garden Clubs of America, 39–40
global warming, 42
Great Basin National Heritage Act (2003), 35–36
Great Basin National Park, 29–32
growth
  rate of, 10–11
  rings on trunk and, 16, 19

habitat, 4
height, 8–9
hieroglyphics, Egyptian, 25–26

insects, 12
Inyo National Forest
  Ancient Bristlecone Pine Forest Botanical Area in, 10, 27, 34, 35
  Schulman and, 19–20, 23

Johnson, LeRoy, 39

Libbey, William, 25
Louth, John, 34, 38

male cones, 7
Methuselah
  cloning of, 37–38
  location of, 34
  Schulman and, 20, 23
  seedlings from, 38, 39–40
Milarch, David, 37
Milarch, Jared, 37, 38, 39
moisture, 4, 10

name, 7
National Geographic (magazine),
  23
National Parks, Board of, 31
needles, 6–7, 10
Nevada, 34
Noren, Al, 19

Patriarch, the
  cloning of, 38
  Schulman and, 19–20
  size of, 9–10
Pauling, Linus, 28–29
Pine Alpha, 20, 34
pinecones, 7, 38, 39
pinus aristata, 7–8
pinus longacva, 8
pinyon pines, 19
pollution, 42
Powell, Doug, 23
Prometheus, 29–32
protection
  cloning and, 37–39
  education and, 29, 31–32
  legislation and, 33–37
  Pauling and, 28–29
  seedlings and, 39–40

radio carbon dating, 24–26
Randel, Joseph T., 28–29
reproduction
  Clark's nutcracker and, 12,
    14–15
  by scientists, 37–40

resin, 10, 12
Rocky Mountain bristlecones,
  8
roots, 10

sap, 10, 12
Schulman, Edmund, 19–20, 23
Schulman Grove, 27
seeds, 12, 14–15
shape, 4, 6
size, 9–10
Snake Mountains (Nevada),
  29–32
Socrates, 29
species, 7–8
Species Survival Commission,
  42
Strybing Arboretum (San
  Francisco), 39
survival traits, 4, 10–12

trunks
  death of, 11–12
  growth rings on, 16, 19
  samples from, 20
  width of, 9–10

United States Department of
  Agriculture (USDA). *See*
  Forest Service
University of Nevada, 31
U.S. Botanical Garden
  (Washington, DC), 39

weather records, 20, 23
Wheeler Peak, 29–32
White Mountains (California),
  10
width, 9–10
Wilderness Act (1964), 33–34,
  35
wildfires, 12
Wild Heritage Act (2002), 35
World Conservation Union, 42

Picture Credits

About the Author

Kelli M. Brucken is the author of many works of nonfiction for children. Her writing has appeared in magazines and newspapers across the country. She enjoys writing about nature, the environment, animals, and history. She makes her home in Auburn, Kansas, with her husband and two children.